MW00412443

SAY GRACE

Daily Reflections on the Goodness of God

Darren Wiley Thomas

This book is dedicated to my three children:
William Chase, Caden Paul and
Claire Annsalyn Thomas.

Jesus is not a myth and His great purpose for
your life is achievable if you will walk with
Him.

"God will instruct you and teach you in the way you should go; He will counsel you and watch over you."

Psalm 32:8

As we look down the road in life there are a lot of questions that hang over our path. What new adventures will we attempt? What great challenges lie ahead? What will bring us joy? What will bring us pain? At the onset of the journey these things are all just mysteries to us, but to the Lord, they are already planned. He already knows each step we will take, each encounter that awaits us along the way. He knows where the path will be smooth. He knows where the path will be steep. He knows when we will run. He knows when we will get tired and He knows when we will fall. The Lord is prepared for the journey. He has packed all of the provisions we will need to survive. He carries all the wisdom we need to make the right decisions. He has packed enough strength to last through every difficulty and He has more courage on hand than we can exhaust. He is fully prepared for our journey, so the only decision that is left for us to make is - will I journey with Him or will I go it alone. Make the decision to go with Him - He has planned the best journey for you.

Dear Jesus,

Help me today to trust your provision in my life and please give me the grace to follow you without reservation. - Amen

"Remove the dross from the silver, and out comes material for the silversmith."

Proverbs 25:4

Let's think about this - is silver silver, with or without the dross? The answer would be - both. Just like a diamond originally lies within the rough rock and gold is buried deep inside the hills, silver has value simply because it is silver. However, its value is not truly revealed until the impurities have been removed. Now let me ask you another question. Are you valuable to God with or without your sins? The answer again is - both. God loves you no matter who you are or where you have been. However, your value is not truly revealed until you trust the blood of Christ to remove your impurities. When you are "polished" by the work of Christ you will see the true beauty of the life God gave you from the beginning. How do I do this? I admit that I have failed God in my life. I believe that His death on the cross was enough to cleanse me from the stain and guilt of sin. I believe that He is alive today. I submit my life to Him. Then - and only then - will my life shine like polished silver.

Dear Jesus,

I know that I have failed in life, I believe that you died on the cross to cancel my sin and that you rose from the dead to conquer sin and death. Jesus today, I give you my life and ask that you polish me for your glory. - Amen

Make this your prayer and the Spirit of God will live inside of you, He will guide you through this life and He will see you through to a home in heaven when you leave this earth.

"The Lord will perfect that which concerns me."

Psalm 138:8

God not only has a plan for our lives, He diligently
works on that plan each day, crafting every detail.
As a painter steps back from his painting and then
steps in again to add just a little more color, God is
forever working on the details of our lives. It may
seem that you are just another product on the
assembly line and that God was only interested in
creating you and spinning you out into the world,
but that is not our God at all. Our God is a loving
creator who continues to "create" us throughout
the course of our lives. He is forever fashioning us
for His great purposes and for His glory. Not only
does He create us, but He also maintains us. He
daily cares for us, provides for us and at times,
disciplines us - all because He loves us. Let Him

guide you, form you, transform you and care for
you today.

Dear Jesus,

**Help me to realize that you not only created
me, but that you also are continually working
on me to make me into the person that you
envisioned from the beginning of time. - Amen**

"Do not conform any longer to the pattern of this world, but be transformed ..."

Romans 12:2

I'm one of those crazy people that actually believes Jesus Christ can change a life. I believe that there is not a hang-up, addiction or vice in our lives that cannot be completely, absolutely and miraculously changed by His hand. It may take time, patience, endurance and pain, but I believe with all my heart that it is possible. If not - the entire Bible is a lie. All of us at some point in our lives have been faced with impossible odds, but that's when we have to revisit the stories of the Bible - blind men that were given sight, outcast sinners that were given new direction and dead men that were given a few more years. Rather than seeing your challenge as being unchangeable - see it as the stage on which a transforming miracle is about to be performed and you have a front row seat.

Dear Jesus,

I believe that you can completely transform a life for the better. Today I give you my life, every part, and I commit to walk in your ways so that I might be changed. - Amen

"Wait on the Lord: be of good courage, and He shall strengthen thine heart . . ."

Psalm 27:14

Do you hate to wait? I know I do. We don't like to wait at red lights because we have places to go and things to do. We don't like to wait in amusement park lines because we want to have fun without being interrupted. We don't like to wait for our dinner because we are hungry. Waiting can really frustrate us. Especially when it is something serious that we are waiting for: healing, a job, a spouse, a child. But it is in the wait that we are forced to sit and talk with God, even if our conversations are strained.

The Psalmist writes, "Wait on the Lord . . .". Waiting is God's way of internally reconstructing us. It gives us the time that we need to evaluate what is most important in life. If we allow Him to, God will change our hearts, our attitudes and our very lives during our most difficult seasons of waiting.

So if you find yourself in the "waiting room" today, be encouraged – the Lord is not asleep, He is working in you, around you, and for you. And when the wait is over you will enjoy the blessing so much more.

Dear Jesus,

I hate to wait, but I know that your timing is perfect. So Jesus, please help me to trust your timing and to wait patiently on your hand. - Amen

"For God is not a God of disorder but of peace."
1 Corinthians 14:33

It is amazing how in contrast the morning news is with the Word of God. When I listen to the daily happenings around the world it seems like total chaos is the norm. But forget the news, sometimes even within my own home things can seem out of control: appointments to meet, bills to be paid, decisions to be made. Sometimes I just feel like sticking my head in the sand. But the Lord is not about chaos. He has a very specific plan for each individual and a very specific plan for each minute of each day. So how do I live in peace in a world that is defined by chaos? I must discipline myself to be still before Him, to listen to His voice and to align every area of my life with Him. Then, and only then, will I be able to stand back and watch order and peace take over.

Dear Jesus,

Sometimes life can seem so out of control. Jesus, please help me to not be frustrated by the chaos in this world and in my life, but rather help me to rest in your sweet presence and perfect peace. - Amen

"'Follow me', Jesus said . . . "

Matthew 4:19

I remember learning how to dive when I was a kid.
My mom would be in the pool saying, "Just jump.",
but I was too afraid to take the risk. My mom had
control of the situation, but she never forced me to
jump in order to teach me how to dive.   We
sometimes use the phrase "God is in control" as an
excuse rather than as a comfort. We wait for God
to force us into something that we know He is
calling us to do.   Yes - God is in control of
everything, but He will not force us to follow Him
in areas where we need to make the move. We say
we are waiting on Him when He may be waiting on
us. He will not bring healing until we seek it, He
will not bring direction until we ask, He will not
bring a new environment to us until we have the
courage to pursue it. What is it that God is asking

you to do today - why are you waiting? God is in control, but He may be waiting for you to jump.

Dear Jesus,

I trust that you are in complete control, but I understand that you will never force me to follow you in obedience. Jesus please give me the courage to follow the instructions that you have already made clear that you would have me to do. - Amen

"They all ate and were satisfied, and the disciples picked up twelve basketfuls of broken pieces that were left over."
Matthew 14:20

When we read the story of Jesus feeding the 5000, we often picture the disciples picking up the leftovers with huge baskets in tow. However, the word "basket" in this passage is translated from the Greek word "kophinas". A kophinas was a smaller basket that was usually strapped over one's shoulder, much like our present day lunch box. So the message we get from Jesus feeding the 5000 is about His *perfect provision.* Jesus fed 5000 plus people and there was just enough left over for the disciples to have lunch. Not too much. Not too little. God had provided just enough to meet all of their needs for the day. God will give us just what we need, when we need it. He is the provider of "our daily bread" not our "annual supply". Don't get ahead of God today - trust Him to provide your need for today. Tomorrow He will do the same.

Dear Jesus,

I get so consumed with worrying about how you will feed me tomorrow that I forget to thank you for the provisions that sit in front of me today. Jesus, please help me to live at peace knowing that you are my provider and that you will meet my every need, today, tomorrow and every day. - Amen

"All of you, clothe yourselves with humility toward one another, because, 'God opposes the proud but gives grace to the humble.'"

1 Peter 5:5

Humility is strength. This has to be the most ironic concept from the Bible. The world says that strength is displayed in getting our way, not letting anyone take advantage of us and speaking our mind in all situations. But the strongest people I know are the most temperate, the least likely to quickly voice their opinion and the first ones to overlook an offense. They are confident in who they are and in their place in life and are not swayed by the opinions and actions of others. They know their God and are content with Him. They are not push-overs or whimps since it takes much more strength to be humble than proud. Jesus had so many enemies and so many critics, but He never fought them. Jesus never had to proudly make a point - He was too busy humbly living a purpose. Don't be deceived by the world's thinking. If you want to be a strong person - put on humility - believe God loves you and has a plan for you - and live an intentional and confident life.

Dear Jesus,

Help me to understand that true strength of character is found in a spirit of humility rather than a spirit of pride. Jesus, please help me to live in such a way that people will want to see me coming rather than run from me because I'm acting like a self-centered grouch. - Amen

"Commit to the Lord whatever you do,
and your plans will succeed."
Proverbs 16:3

I commit this day to the Lord - not tomorrow, not next week, not next year for they are too far away to concern me.

I commit this day to the Lord - forgetting yesterday, last week and last year for they cannot be changed nor altered.

I commit this day to the Lord - for it is the only day that I can truly experience His presence working in me.

I commit this day to the Lord - I refuse to live it in fear, resentment or shame.

I commit this day to the Lord - acknowledging that
I cannot control the actions of others,
but I can control my own reactions.

I commit this day to the Lord - for I know His
plans for me are greater, higher and more perfect
than anything I could plan for myself.

I commit this day to the Lord - for He committed
Himself to the cross for me.

I commit this day to the Lord.

Dear Jesus,

**In the best way I know how - I commit this day
to you.   - Amen**

"... he who hates correction is stupid."

Proverbs 12:1

You can't get much more to the point than that.
Why do we have to always feel that we are right?
When cars drive slow in front of us we get
frustrated because they are holding us up. When
cars race around us we fuss at them for driving
unsafe. When the house is not clean, it is the kids'
fault. When the project at work does not turn out
right, it is your colleagues fault. Why can't
everyone in the world get it right?! I seem to have
no problem. Well - the problem with everyone else
is that they are limited, fallen individuals - and
when I am living in reality - so am I. I would do
well to remember that. So there will be times when
my wife asks me to do something that I have not
been doing that I probably should respect. There

will be times when my boss asks me to do something a little bit differently and I should take his advice. And there will be times when the spirit of God will call for me to make an adjustment in my life and I should heed His instructions. Don't be stupid - welcome correction into your life.

Dear Jesus,

Please help me to have a teachable spirit today. Help me to recognize that being corrected from time to time is actually a good thing that ends up working in my favor in the long run. - Amen

"But the greatest of these is love."

1 Corinthians 13:13

If the apostle Paul had been from south Georgia I think 1 Corinthians 13 would sound something like this - "If I can preach a good sermon or teach a good Bible lesson, but not love the people I teach - I'm just doing it to hear myself and it means nothin'. If I tote my Bible, listen to Christian radio, hang a fish on the back of my car, post messages about God on Facebook and go to church every now and then, but hate my family instead of love them, then I'm nothin'. If I give money to the local mission, drop a few dollars in the plate on Sunday and maybe even help a homeless man find a meal, but do it out of obligation and not real love - well - you get the picture. Love is patient with people that are impatient, love is nice to people that are not nice to it, it does not hate when others succeed, it does not brag, it is not puffed up, it is not mouthy. Love does not try to always get it's way, it doesn't get ticked easily and it doesn't hold grudges. Love does not happily indulge in the things God says are wrong, but instead joyfully celebrates following God's way. Love always protects, always trusts, always hopes, always perseveres. You just can't go wrong with real love- it's the true evidence of whether I know God or not."

Dear Jesus,

When I observe your ways, I see true love. You have truly loved me when I did not deserve it. Jesus, help me to realize today that true love is a choice that I make – an attitude I must chose to embrace. Help me to love the way that you love. - Amen

". . . and it came to pass, when the people heard the sound of the trumpet, and the people shouted with a great shout, that the wall fell down flat, so that the people went up into the city, every man straight before him, and they took the city."

Joshua 6:20 (KJV)

After the death of Moses, God called Joshua to step up to the plate and lead the Israelites into the Promised Land, but there was a big obstacle standing in their way – the city of Jericho. Jericho was positioned in such a way that there was no traveling around it, under it, nor over it. The only way to the Promised Land was THROUGH Jericho and the only way through it was through it's massive walls. So God tells Joshua and the Israelites to march around the city walls for seven days. On the seventh day, God commanded them to march around the walls seven more times and then to blow a trumpet. Only then would the walls fall. Joshua obeyed and what God promised came true. After the seventh march and the blowing of the trumpet, the walls of Jericho did not just crumble or topple, the Bible says the walls fell down "flat". Some archeologists believe that the walls fell in such a way that they paved the way for the Israelites to enter into the city. Isn't that just like God to take our greatest obstacles and turn them into a highway of victory. If you find yourself facing a wall of sorts today, be patient, God is in the business of turning our obstacles into opportunities and our barriers into highways to a life of higher purpose. Don't let your obstacles scare you, submit them to the Lord and one day you will be walking on them.

Dear Jesus,

Today I will face every obstacle in my path with great faith, knowing that by your power you will provide a way through it.   - Amen

"Is anyone among you suffering? Let him pray."

James 5:13

Read that again. - - Read it one more time. Now, based on what James says in this verse, who is to be the first to pray when you find yourself in trouble? You. "Is anyone ...suffering? Let HIM pray." Too often we farm out our responsibility to pray. Not that it is wrong to ask others to pray for us. We need to do that. The Bible is clear in many places that we are to pray for others and that we are to ask others to pray for us. However, sometimes we neglect our responsibility to pray for ourselves when we are in need. Maybe we have a lack of confidence in our prayers, maybe we feel like we just don't know how to pray. Whatever the case, God is not concerned with our methods as much as He is concerned with our faith. Any prayer directed to the Lord is an act of faith, no matter how big or small, no matter how eloquent or broken. Are you in trouble today? If so, you be the one to go to the throne of God first on your own behalf and then ask others to support you. In doing so, you exhibit the act of faith that God will honor. Don't fear prayer, fear a life without it. Pray for yourself.

Dear Jesus,

I need you today to encourage my heart with your presence and through your Word. I need your help, your guidance and your hope in my own life before I can ever be of any help to others. Jesus, please meet the specific needs of my life and carry me through this day for your glory. - Amen

"You intended it to harm me,
but God intended it for good."

Genesis 50:20

Difficulties are not the work of God. Why is it that each time we go through a difficult time, we look toward heaven and say "WHY ARE YOU DOING THIS TO ME GOD?!" Keep in mind, God created a world void of trouble and pain. It was man that made the choice to disobey God. Man's disobedience resulted in brokenness and pain. God did not invent slavery. He is the one who came up with a plan to deliver the Israelites from slavery. God did not put malice into the hearts of Joseph's brothers, but He did pave the way to Joseph's prosperity after he had been betrayed. God didn't take everything from Job, but He gave Satan permission to test a man that He knew would lean on Him for strength. In every trial of life - let's be clear - God is not the author of pain, but He is the great deliverer who can turn our pain into triumph. Difficulties are not the work of God, but they are the canvas on which He paints the purpose of our lives.

Dear Jesus,

I'm sorry for the times I have blamed you for the difficulties in my life. I am sorry for the times that I failed to see your loving hand guiding me through those times. Please help me today to see every difficult experience as an opportunity to see your power revealed. - Amen

"The Lord is the stronghold of my life."

Psalm 27:1

There are so many negative strongholds that cripple us from really experiencing the peace of God in our lives: worry, anger, fear, lust, addictions. The list can go on and on. When we seek to conquer all of these on our own, we fail miserably and we live in constant defeat and discouragement. But when we realize who we are in Christ, that we have already been forgiven of all our sins, that we are a child of God, that we are secure in Him, that His power lives inside of us, that it is all about Him and none about me - then we begin to experience freedom, strength and peace. Too often we try to live the Christian life without Christ and it leaves us defeated. Today, Christ is my stronghold. He is the one I cling to, trust in and by the power of the Spirit will be controlled by. Let Him have all of you today and find His peace.

Dear Jesus,

I am powerless without you. I need you every minute of every day. With you I am able to overcome the monsters that seek to slay me. With you I have power, purpose and hope. Thank you for not leaving me alone. - Amen

"He got up, rebuked the wind and said to the waves, 'Quiet! Be still!' Then the wind died down and it was completely calm."

Mark 4:39

No doubt the disciples had tried to weather this storm at first without waking Jesus. As they traveled across the Sea of Galilee, with Jesus sleeping in the hull of the boat, the wind starts to pick up and the waves start white capping. I imagine the first inclination of the disciples was to lower the sails and start securing their equipment. All while letting Jesus sleep. I picture Peter barking out orders for the others to row faster, to bail the water out of the boat and to HOLD ON! All while letting Jesus sleep. Finally it dawns on someone, "Will somebody wake up Jesus?!". In other words, "We've done all that we know to do and this storm is too big for us!" So they wake up

Jesus. I wonder, why did they not wake Him up sooner? After all, He was the only one that had the ability to calm the storm. Jesus wakes up and settles the storm and asks the disciples, "Why are you so afraid? Do you still have no faith?" I believe this is Jesus' way of saying, "Why was I your last resort? Why didn't you come to me sooner?". The good news for us is that God does not sleep and is ever watchful over us. The bad news is we forget that truth. If you are walking through a storm today, trust the ability of Jesus to take care of you and go to Him first. It will save you a whole lot of panic.

Dear Jesus,

I pray I never come to you as a last resort, having made a mess of things by trying to walk it alone. Jesus, help me to run to you first with every sign of high winds and rippling waves. - Amen

"... your joy will be complete."
Deuteronomy 16:15

One of the feasts celebrated by the Israelites was called The Feast of Tabernacles. This was a time to celebrate the harvest as well as a time to remember and celebrate how the Lord had provide for them and protected them while they wandered the desert for 40 years. It was a celebration of deliverance. The Lord promised them that celebrating His provision and their deliverance would make their joy "complete". We have a promised land of our own that awaits us because of the deliverance offered to us through the shed blood of Christ on the cross. Therefore, our joy is made complete. Real joy is the inner satisfaction that my every need has been met by Christ, that I have been protected from the wrath of God displayed on the cross and that my deepest spiritual needs are met by His presence. You cannot have genuine joy without salvation. You may have happiness, but it will be conditional on someone or something. Just like you can't have honey without bees, you can't experience true joy without experiencing the cleansing grace of God. Have you lost your joy? Take a moment to remind yourself where you would be without Christ then reflect on how He has totally forgiven all of your mistakes and loves you. And just like that, JOY will return.

Dear Jesus,

I praise you today that I have been delivered from the curse of sin. Though I still struggle, I know that I have been completely and wonderfully forgiven by you for all the wrongs that I have done. Jesus, help me this day to walk in the joy of my salvation. - Amen

"Love your neighbor as yourself."

Mark 12:31

Loving others - Jesus called it the second greatest commandment after loving God. That sounds so weak, so mushy, so girly. Shouldn't the second greatest commandant be witnessing or standing against evil or studying God's Word? How about spending time in prayer, building churches or feeding the poor? Why all this mushy love stuff? Jesus taught that loving others must come first or none of these other things can happen with sincerity. Love is anything but mushy and weak. You see love is a choice - and it's a tough choice. It is not an emotion that we mysteriously experience, it is a conscious decision that we make to value our fellow man. When we chose to treat people with value, be they our friends or our enemies, we show respect for God and His creation. When we chose to love, no matter how we feel, we prove that God lives inside of us. The discipline of love is not for sissies, it is for men and women who are determined to live surrendered to the desires of God over their own desires. It truly is the greatest challenge given to mankind and it can only be done by the power of God working through people who are most surrendered to Him. That, my friends, is strength. That, my friends, is God.

Dear Jesus,

Help me to see each person I encounter as a person created in your image, a person that you love, a person for whom you have a plan. Jesus, help me to love others the way that you have loved me – totally unconditionally. - Amen

"For all that is in the world—the desires of the flesh and the desires of the eyes and pride of life —is not from the Father but is from the world."

1 John 2:16

You are boarding a plane for a long flight over the Atlantic Ocean. You enter the plane, take your seat and over the PA system you hear from the cockpit, "Good afternoon ladies and gentleman this is captain 'Feelings'. I would like to welcome you aboard Emotions Airline. Our destination today will be wherever we feel like it once we get into the air. We may experience some turbulents along the way in the event that anything makes me mad this morning. You may or may not get a meal depending on how the crew feels about serving you today. In the event of an emergency just do your best to follow your gut on how to survive. We hope you enjoy your flight today aboard Emotions Airline." We would not trust feelings to control a flight, why would we trust feelings to control our lives? Do what you know to be true from the Word of God today and trust the Lord, not your feelings. It's the only way to have a safe landing.

Dear Jesus,

Feelings are so powerful over me. So often I make decisions based upon how I feel, rather than on the solid instruction given to me from your Word. Jesus, help me today to be guided by your Spirit and not by the inconsistent emotions that lie within me. - Amen

"Speak, Lord, for your servant is listening."

1 Samuel 3:10

90% of communication problems happen because we use our mouths more than we use our ears. When the mouth is used more than the ear, marriages fracture, friendships crumble and organizations break into chaos. But when we actually discipline ourselves to actively listen to the other party we gain understanding for ourselves and also respect from the other person. What is it that God is trying to tell us today, but we are too busy talking to Him, asking of Him and pleading with Him to hear? There is a time and place for "making our request known to God", but then there is even more a time and place to be quiet and still in order to listen to Him. Many years ago a good friend taught me that it is essential in the

Christian life to pick a time to meet with God, pick a place where you will be uninterrupted and then to just be still and listen. God has answers to give you today. Don't do all the talking. We miss many answers because we continue asking questions without pause.

Dear Jesus,

Today I just want to hear your voice. Help me to use my ears and heart more than my mouth during my times of prayer so that I might hear the depths of your love for me. - Amen

"The way of the Lord is a refuge for the righteous."
Proverbs 10:29

Webster defines "refuge" as "shelter or protection from danger or distress". When a physical storm comes our way we are instructed to find *refuge* in a small room in the center of our house. This is usually found in a small bathroom or closet. These small spaces are said to be the safest place in the house, the area that is least likely to be affected by the high winds and flying debris. But what if the storm is spiritual or emotional? Then where do we go for refuge? God's Word reminds us that the commandments of the Lord are our safety zone. Walking in His ways do not prevent the spiritual storms from raging any more than locking ourselves in a bathroom will stop the physical storm from ripping shingles off our roof. However, daily committing ourselves to seeking the Lord and living in line with His Word will put us in a refuge of emotional and spiritual safety and rest that cannot be found anywhere else. Don't try to weather the emotional and spiritual storms of life out in the open on your own. Huddle down in the Word of God and find refuge.

Dear Jesus,

The winds are howling all around us. Help us to lock ourselves into your presence and your Word today to experience your peace. - Amen

"A patient man has great understanding,
but a quick tempered man displays folly."

Proverbs 14:29

We often hear people say, "Don't pray for patience or God will test you in order for you to learn it." How crazy is that?! That's like saying, "Don't pray for God to provide your family with food or He'll make you starve in order for you to appreciate the food you have." God is not cruel in giving gifts to His children. He is eager to display His power in our lives. So when we ask Him to surpass our human abilities, He is quick to answer. I don't know about you, but I can be very impatient - and unfortunately I am usually the most impatient with the ones I love the most. So if I know I need help, why in the world would I not ask God to help me. I'm certainly not going to find help for my inadequacies anywhere else. If God can't give me patience, there is no hope. It is not a skill to be learned. Patience is a fruit of the Holy Spirit that is in contrast to my natural instincts. Therefore, I need the Lord to give it to me.

Dear Jesus,

Help me to be patient today with everyone I encounter, because without your help I can be a real jerk. - Amen

"Therefore, if anyone is in Christ, he is a new creation; the old has gone, the new has come!"

2 Corinthians 5:17

Have you ever dropped a rock into a river and watched it quickly disappear from sight until it was gone? Have you ever released a balloon and watched it slowly drift into the clouds until it was gone? When something is "gone" it is never to be reclaimed again. It's near impossible to pull the rock up from the bottom of the river and you'll never reclaim that balloon from the clouds. The Apostle Paul reminds us that when we place our faith in Christ we are brand new creations, something totally new. He reminds us that the old has "gone" – never to be reclaimed again. But I still sin and struggle with sin, so has the old really gone? In the eyes of God it has. You are hidden in

Christ. When God looks at you He sees the nature of His Son. As much as we struggle to fight the flesh, the great truth of the gospel is this - for those who trust Christ, our old nature cannot be reclaimed - it is GONE!

Dear Jesus,

Sometimes I do not feel like a new creation. Please help me today to live in the peace of knowing that when you look at me, you see your own nature living in me. Remind me that the old me is gone and you have taken over. - Amen

"God showed his love for us in this way.
Christ died for us while we were sinners."

Romans 5:8

To get a pay check, you have to work hard to earn it. To get a mate, you must do something to impress them. To get a trophy, you must discipline yourself to win above the others. But, to get God to love you, you have to do absolutely nothing. That's right - absolutely NOTHING. The greatest mystery of all time is how a loving Holy God could love us when we are filthy. I say "are filthy" for a reason. I don't know about you - but I know that I still struggle with sin after 33 years of being a Christian. But it's because of God's great love that I seek to live holy. Holy living begins with an understanding that I am naturally an unholy person. That is what motivates me to obey. We

52

seek to live holy as an expression of worship to the One who loves us unconditionally and has made us clean. God loves you no matter what you do – now let what you do reflect how much God loves you.

Dear Jesus,

How such a Holy God could love such an unholy man is a mystery to me, but I know that it is true. Thank you Jesus for loving me, no matter what. Now, please help me today to live in such a way that thanks you for the love that you have given me. - Amen

"My soul clings to you."

Psalm 63:8

Desperation is a good thing. It is the tension of desperate times that causes us to seek security and answers in life. Without these times of desperation we would go through life never learning, growing or becoming. Desperation should lead us to a deeper dependence on the Lord, but often desperation causes us to question His presence and His power. When desperate times come, we must call on our Heavenly Father for help. I like the fact that my kids depend on me. I like it when they say, "Daddy can you open this jar?" "Daddy will you fix my toy?" "Daddy I miss you." When our hearts are desperate we are vulnerable and aware that we need someone or something outside of ourselves to help us. So why do we mourn desperate times?

Well, of course, because they hurt. However, pain is often the prescription that leads to a healthier, happier, more fulfilling life in the end. If you are living in desperate times today, go to your Heavenly Father and ask Him to help you. He will care for you and you will love Him all the more for it.

Dear Jesus,

I'm living in a desperate time. Things seem to be out of control, but I know that you are able to care for all of my needs. Jesus, please help me with the desperate places of my life. I trust you. - Amen

"If God is for us, who can be against us?"

Romans 8:31

Does it frustrate you that others don't seem to get you? Does it bother you that those around you know your name, your family, your job and your hobbies, but they just don't seem to know your fears, your hurts or even your dreams? Well, there is one who knows you beyond anyone else and He knows you completely. More than your friends, your children, your spouse, your parents or even yourself, Almighty God knows you, and guess what . . . He is on your side. Not "on your side" in the sense that He wants to leave you to your own devices or condone your rebellious tendencies. But "on your side" in the sense that He gets you, He understands you, He loves you. Nothing you do, and nothing anyone else can do, will ever change that. The creator of all that is good and holy loves you, what could possibly stand against that?

Dear Jesus,

Sometimes it feels that the world is against me and that no one can understand what is going on in my head and my heart. Thank you for loving me and knowing me even better than I know myself. - Amen

"Do not be wise in your own eyes;
fear the Lord and shun evil."
Proverbs 3:7

When I was a child, my mama used this saying any time I acted as if I knew better than her - "You're just too big for your britches." That was her way of saying, "You are not always right and you might want to step back and learn a thing or two." Sometimes I run into people that are "too big for their britches", highly intelligent, but very unwise. Knowing things and knowing God are two totally different concepts. Being able to debate well is not the same thing as being able to love well. An immoral mind is often confused as an open mind. An arrogant man is sometimes mistaken for a wise man. Since the beginning of time man has been trying to use the "Intelligence Card" to trump the wisdom and will of God. Don't make the same mistake. Put on the "britches" that fit you and trust that the Lord is right in all that He says in His Word.

Dear Jesus,

Unfortunately there are times when I think I know better than anyone else. There are even times when my actions show that I think I know better than you because I choose to do the opposite of what you say. Dear Jesus, please help me not to live "too big for my britches". Help me to live teachable, humble and true. - Amen

"Enter through the narrow gate because the gate and road that lead to destruction are wide."

Matthew 7:13

If you were in a burning building, would you trust the doors that read "In Case of Emergency Exit Here" or would you choose another route? If you were on a sinking ship, would you follow the signs leading you to the deck where there were life boats or would you instead try to swim your way to shore? No- in both of these situations, we would trust the experts. We would follow the predetermined way of escape. So why do we try to find life and peace in any other avenue than the great invitation of love and grace given to us by Jesus Christ- the expert on life. Jesus is not arrogant in His invitation to say that He is the only way. On the contrary - He is humble. Jesus made

Himself nothing and took the punishment for our sins so that we could be free and find life. Now He simply invites us to trust Him and follow. Even when everyone else may seem to move in the other direction, make the choice to follow Christ. The way to peace and life is narrow - it is the width of one person, Jesus Christ and we cannot walk through it unless we are walking behind Him.

Dear Jesus,

I cannot help myself, forgive my sin and help me to follow you. Today I choose your narrow, but certain, way. - Amen

"Whatever your hand finds to do,
do it with all your might . . ."
Ecclesiastes 9:10

There is a difference between good and great. There is a difference between getting by and getting it right. There is a difference between doing something just to get it done and doing something with excellence. The difference is found in who you do it for. If you go to work just to get a paycheck you may not really care what kind of job you do, but if you go to work giving thanks to God that you have a job that provides income for your family then you may work more diligently in thanksgiving to God. If you care for your family because you feel like no one else is going to do it you may grow resentful, but if you care for your family with the understanding that God has placed those lives around you to learn from you about His great love, then you may be more inclined to see the impact of a Godly mother, father, brother, sister, son, daughter. Whatever you do today, do it for your real boss, the Lord. He provides a great benefits package.

Dear Jesus,

Please help me to live a life of service, not out of obligation, but rather out of a privilege to be a part of your excellent work on earth. - Amen

"Set your minds on things above, not on earthly things."
Colossians 3:2

You did a lot of things intentionally this morning to get ready for your day. You intentionally fixed your breakfast, brushed your teeth and ironed your clothes. You may have intentionally fed the dog, woke the kids, or paid some bills. All these things, you made a choice to do. If you had not chosen to do them, they would have gone undone. God invites us to a place of peace and emotional stability when we intentionally CHOOSE to SET our minds on Him. When we take the initiative to intentionally respond to His invitation we will find that our lives are transformed for the better. When we live with intention we are no longer victims to circumstance and emotion. We actually have a say in what we allow into our minds and our emotions. Take a minute right now and intentionally set your mind on the Lord. If you do, you will find a peace and security that you did not know existed.

Dear Jesus,

So often I let my feelings and my circumstances control my day. Jesus, right now I intentionally set my mind on the fact that you love me unconditionally and that you have a great purpose for my life. Help me to keep my thoughts set on you throughout the day. - Amen

"There is a way that seems right to a man,
but in the end it leads to destruction."
Proverbs 14:12

I was watching a safety video for work the other day and it showed an office chair and said, "This is not a ladder." I thought, "Well of course not." Then, just a couple of days later I was hanging a picture in my office and I did not have a ladder. So what did I do? You got it - I pulled up a chair and balanced myself to hang the picture. I nearly broke my neck getting down. God gives us instructions for our safety, but we always seem to think that those instructions are optional. We like to talk about the instructions and even teach the instructions, but when it comes to following them it is often just a matter of convenience to us. Unfortunately, we try to take short cuts when it comes to obeying God. Rather than fully trusting

His commands, we compromise and it ends up hurting us. When it comes to reaching new heights, office chairs are not an option and disobeying the teachings of the Bible are not either.

Dear Jesus,

Help me to realize that every verse of Scripture is written for my own good. Please help me to live the Scriptures by the power of your Spirit, so that I may keep from breaking my own neck. - Amen

"Let us go over to the other side."

Mark 4:35

Jesus told his disciples to get into a boat so that they could "go over to the other side" and they willingly jumped in thinking they were in for a leisurely ride across the lake. But, sometime in the journey they were met with an unexpected storm. The winds were tearing at their sails and the waves were crashing over the bow. They were terrified, but Jesus was completely calm. As a matter of fact, he was taking a nap through the whole ordeal. In a panic the disciples woke him up. "Teacher, don't you care?!" they shouted. Without any great ceremony, Jesus spoke and the seas calmed down, then he asked them "Why are you so afraid? Do you still have no faith?" God often calls us to pre-storm commitments. If we saw all the storms up front, we may never be willing to get into the boat with Him. But once we are in, we can be assured that if Jesus said we are going to the other side, then He will see that we get there safely. Trust Jesus today. He will get you through your storm. He will see that you safely sink your toes into the sands of His preordained destination for your life.

Dear Jesus,

When the waves start crashing and the winds pick up, please help me to remember that you are the captain of more than the ship, you are the captain of the sea and the storm as well.
- Amen

"If any of you lacks wisdom, let him ask of God who gives to all liberally."

James 1:5

Is there really any reason why we as believers should not be able to make very wise decisions in life? Wisdom is not something that is just meant for a select few. Wisdom is available to all. God allows us to borrow His wisdom while we walk this earth. Wisdom is not our way of thinking or reasoning. If that were the case we would all be in a mess. No - wisdom is simply thinking the way God thinks and the only way for us to do that is to ask Him. The only wisdom that we do not possess is the wisdom we refuse to request. God has made His wisdom accessible to us, but honestly when was the last time you asked the Lord to grant you wisdom? Whatever decisions you face today, don't sweat it - just ask God for His wisdom - He is waiting and eager to give it.

Dear Jesus,

Please give me your wisdom today to deal with every situation I face according to your will. - Amen

"You who seek God, your hearts shall live."

Psalm 69:32

We seek so many things in life that do not bring life. Oh - they sound good; things like happiness, peace, health, contentment. We seek all of these things hoping that they will bring us a meaningful and fulfilling life. The irony of it all is that these are the things that God desires for us to have, but when we make them the object of our affections and try to maneuver our lives in order to get them, we never find them. God never says to seek happiness, peace, health or contentment in order to find life. No - He simply says, "Seek Me" and when we do all of those other things just naturally happen.

Dear Jesus,

Sometimes it seems that life is nothing more than a continual cycle of seeking the next thing that will bring me satisfaction, contentment or happiness. Jesus, today I choose to make you all that I seek and to find my contentment in you. - Amen

"Your word is a lamp to my feet and
a light to my path."
Psalm 119:105

The thing about a lamp is that it does not light up the room next to you, only the room you are in. Even if the lamp is in the room with you, you can't read a book very well if the lamp you are using is across the room, you have to sit under it. You'll never see a lamp strapped onto the front of a car or hoisted up to the top of a ship to cast light out into the distance. No - a lamp is just to shed light for a few steps and that's all. God has a great plan for your life, but you will never find it if you keep straining to see past the light of His lamp (His Word). God has given us His Word to not only teach us about Himself, but to help us walk through life with clear direction. Spend some time in the Scriptures today and let Him shed light onto your next step. When you get there, He'll show you the next.

Dear Jesus,

I get so anxious about the things that may lie on the path far ahead of me. Jesus, please help me to realize that the only step that should concern me is the next one. Help me to learn from your Word what that step should be and give me the courage to take it. – Amen

"Where your treasure is, there your heart will be also."
Matthew 6:21

In the summer of 2013 our family was in the process of packing up all of our things to prepare for a major move from Georgia to North Carolina. There were some things that we just threw in a box without any real worries of whether it would make it or not to the new destination. But, then there were other items that were wrapped in bubble wrap, double wrapped in paper and carefully placed into a sturdy box and cushioned again with more paper. Those carefully packed items had more personal value - the clay handprints of our kids, the Christmas ornament bought in New York, the brittle Bibles of our grandparents. We packed them carefully because each piece represents a piece of our heart.

If you had one box to pack today with the greatest of care, what would you put in it? Whatever you would place in that box, that is where your heart is.

Dear Jesus,

Help me to never treasure anything more than I treasure you. - Amen

"But you, O Lord, are a compassionate and gracious
God, slow to anger . . ."
Psalm 86:15

For centuries humanity has lived as if God were out to get us - as if He were some cruel step-father that really does not love us and is waiting to smite us for all of our weaknesses and failures. However, the Bible is clear that God is SLOW to anger. In other words, He would not lose His cool in traffic, He would let others go ahead of Him in the check-out line, He would never scream at His kids nor argue with family. God does not get mad easily. I so deserve to be struck by lightning and left in a pile of ashes on a daily basis, but God is "slow to anger and abounding in love". He is patient with us, loving toward us, and wants us to know that He is approachable. God loves us - even when we walk

away from Him, He patiently waits for our return.
He is slow to condemn, quick to forgive. You don't
want to refuse that kind of acceptance.

Dear Jesus,

**Thank you for being patient with me. Thank
you for extending your loving hand to me when
I least deserve it. Help me to live in such a way
that shows you how grateful I am for your love.
- Amen**

"'For I know the plans I have for you', says the Lord."
Jeremiah 29:11

When you and I board an airplane, we are at the mercy of the pilot. We know nothing about what happens in that cockpit, but we trust that the pilot knows the plan. Our faith is not in the flight plan, but rather in the pilot's ability to carry out the plan. Our safety and destination are in His hands. When we read Jeremiah 29:11 we often jump to the word "plan", finding comfort in the fact that God has a plan and purpose for us. However, I have come to find great comfort in the words "I KNOW" from this great verse. It's great to know that there is a divine plan for my life, but it's even more comforting to know that Amighty God is the one who has fashioned that plan and by His divine power, He will see it through. God never called anyone to seek His plan, instead He calls us only to seek Him. Lord, help me today to avoid seeking the plan, but instead, help me to seek You. Then I can know that I will have a safe landing.

Dear Jesus,

I want so desperately to know your plan, but I will never know your plan if I do not know you. Jesus, help me to seek you and to trust you with your plan for my life. - Amen

"But unless you repent, you too will perish."
Luke 13:5

The word "repent" gets really bad press. We see street corner preachers shouting it from a bull horn and think "how insensitive". We shy away from using the word for fear that others will think that we are being judgmental or unloving. But "repentance" actually brings peace. When I was about 11 years old I remember lying in my bed very upset. I thought I had messed up and lost my salvation. I had only been a Christian a short while, but I obviously felt guilty and afraid over something I had done. My mother came into my room and asked me what was bothering me. I explained my fear to her. She sat down on the edge of my bed and explained that once we are saved, sin does not separate us from God again, but God does wants us to "repent" of it – confess it and turn from it - so that we can have peace. We prayed together and I went off to sleep like a baby - never worried about it again. Sin cannot make God stop loving us, but it can steal our peace. If you have made a mistake that haunts you, don't fear repentance, embrace it. Confess your failure to God, turn from your failure into a new direction and accept His free grace. You will sleep like a baby.

Dear Jesus,

Feelings of guilt, shame and condemnation are not from you. Please help me to not live in the shadow of my mistakes, but rather to live in the light of your grace. - Amen

"What good is it for someone to gain the whole world,
yet forfeit their soul?"

Mark 8:36

My 92 year old grandmother lived in the same house for nearly 70 years. She had a 4x4 closet in her bedroom, her kitchen cabinets were held shut with wooden spoons and her washing machine was on the back porch. Yet, her cookie jar was always full of cookies, her yard was always full of flowers and her bills were always paid. She never sought to gain the things of the world. She simply sought to survive in it by faith and to be content with what she had. She has been in heaven now for over two years, but her impact on our family is still strong. She was rich in the things that mattered: faith, family and friends. What are we living for today? Let's not miss the point of life, let's seek to live for the things that matter. The only way to truly make a difference in the world is to never focus on this world, but rather the world to come - then and only then will we be remembered. Then and only then will we be rich.

Dear Jesus,

Help me today to focus on the things that matter: Faith, Family and Friends and to let all other things take a far second place. - Amen

"And my God will meet all your needs . . ."
Philippians 4:19

Are you worried about money this morning? Are you concerned that you cannot find a job? Are you looking for a friend or maybe even a spouse to share life with you? Are you waiting for a baby to come into your family? All of us look ahead and wonder "How will it work out?" "When will the answer come?" "Where is the solution?" If this is you today, you are no alone. We all have times of looking down the road and wondering what is ahead. It's at these times that we must look over our shoulder and list all of the blessings and provisions that God has already brought into our lives. Make a mental scrapbook of all that God has done to bless you in the past and you will find faith to take the next step into the future. He is faithful - He will meet our every need. Trust Him and relax.

Dear Jesus,

I spend so much time worrying about what will happen tomorrow that I do not take time to reflect on your faithfulness for today. Please help me to live grateful, thankful and faithful. - Amen

"Do I seek to please men? For if I still pleased men,
I would not be a bondservant of Christ."
Galatians 1:10

People pleasing - what a disease. Many of us suffer
from it. Some people even claim, "I don't care what
others think about me!" in an attempt to impress
others of their strength. Again worrying about
what others think. So much of our life is wasted on
worrying about what others will say and think
about us. It affects the way we dress in high school,
the car we drive in college, the house we buy early
on in life. It can cause us to try and be something
we are not created to be in order to impress, or at
the very least, find acceptance from those around
us. Sometimes worrying about pleasing men causes
us to make decisions that do not please God - and
He is the one that really cares about our well-being

more than anyone. So today - live for the audience of one, God alone, and seek to please Him. It will bring you the most satisfaction.

Dear Jesus,

Help me today to be focused only upon you and what you think rather than the opinions and expectations of others. - Amen

"If anyone is thirsty, let him come to me and drink."

John 7:37

Both of my sons play baseball. Before every game or practice, we always ask "Do you have a drink?". Powerade, water, whatever it may be - they always keep some liquid in their bag. This is not for their pleasure, it is for their survival. In the summer heat, a drink is necessary. Without it they will get sick, weak and will not be able to play in the game. They have to stay hydrated to stay healthy and to play hard. Jesus tells us that if we want to stay spiritually healthy and strong, we have to stay "hydrated" with His Spirit as we drink from His Word. We cannot expect to perform at our best without His sustaining power at work within us. If we ignore His Word, we will soon find ourselves on the sidelines gasping for spiritual strength. So before you "hit the field" today let me ask you "have you had a drink" from the life sustaining Word of God? If not, take a minute and get "hydrated" – it will improve your game 100%.

Dear Jesus,

Help me to be as dependent on your Word as I would be dependent on a drink of water in the heat of summer. - Amen

"For we are God's workmanship, created in Christ Jesus to do good works, which God prepared in advance for us to do."

Ephesians 2:10

Remember Geppetto, the carpenter that made Pinocchio? While he chiseled and shaved and painted the little boy puppet, he imagined all that the little puppet would be and do to entertain others. Even after Pinocchio came to life and began to make decisions that got him into trouble, Geppetto kept pursuing him until Pinocchio was back home and fulfilling the purpose of his creator. God has created you with a specific purpose in mind. While he was forming you, he was forming you with specific talents and gifts in order to fulfill what He has planned for your life. You are no mistake, you are not just one among many. You are

specifically fashioned by God "to do good works".
No matter who you are or where you have been,
you can come home to God's purpose for your life.
Pinocchio discovered that there is no better place
for a puppet to be than in the hands of his creator.
It is only then that he could be and do what he was
made to be and do. Pinocchio was happiest in the
hands of Geppetto - think about that.

Dear Jesus,

**Your plans for me are far better than any plans
that I might have for my own life. Please help
me to remember that I have been created by
you, that you know what is best for me and that
I will be most content in your hands. - Amen**

"My thoughts are not your thoughts . . . "
Isaiah 55:8

When I read these words of the Lord through the prophet Isaiah I think to myself, "THANK GOD!" If God's thoughts were like my thoughts then He would often be confused, afraid and uncertain. But His thoughts are confident, peaceful, certain and good. Today, be reminded that Almighty God loves you and that He has great plans for your life. He is "thinking" good things for you. I know there are times when you feel like He is not listening or paying attention, but be assured that He loves you and He desires what is best for you. He will carry you as you trust that He is not out to get you, but rather out to guide you. Learn to "think" like Him and rest.

Dear Jesus,

I am so glad that you do not think like me. I am even more grateful that you give me the opportunity to take on your thoughts so that I might live in peace. Jesus, please help me to think your thoughts instead of my own and to find my security in you. - Amen

"Abraham called that place The Lord Will Provide."

Genesis 22:14

What an agonizing story. God told Abraham to take his beloved son up a mountain and sacrifice him as a burnt offering. God was testing Abraham's devotion. It's as if two chairs were set before Abraham, in one sat his son and the other God. God asked Abraham to choose. Abraham chose God over his own son. Oh the agony! With determination to put God first, Abraham trod up that mountain grieving what seemed to be the demise of his child. God on the other hand was celebrating the blessings that were in store. Because Abraham chose God over his own son, God blessed him and honored them both and Abraham's son, Isaac was spared. The hand of God was now on both of their lives and their descendants were blessed. Nowhere in the Bible does it say to put our children first. Instead God commands us to put Him first, to trust Him and to honor Him. When we do, our children in turn are blessed. When we don't, they are cursed. The best thing I can do for my children is to prioritize them behind the will of God and to trust His purpose for their lives.

Dear Jesus,

This is a hard lesson to learn – that my children do not come first. Help me to align myself to your purposes and then to trust my children to your care. - Amen

"But the fruit of the Spirit is love, joy, peace, patience, kindness, goodness, faithfulness, gentleness and self-control."

Galatians 5:22

Sometimes when I go out to our farm I see deer tracks in the field. They are very distinctive. They do not look like dog prints, bear prints or elephant prints-they are distinctively deer prints. The marks of a Christian are very distinctive. They have nothing to do with knowledge, intellect, reason or strength. The marks of a Christian leave the people they encounter wanting to experience more. What kind of tracks are you leaving today? Make it your aim to leave the marks of love, joy, peace, patience, kindness, goodness, faithfulness, gentleness and self-control. Being a Christian is not about who you profess, but rather who possesses you.

Dear Jesus,

I pray my life might be defined by these evidences of your presence in my life:

Love

Joy

Peace

Patience

Kindness

Goodness

Faithfulness

Gentleness

Self-control

By your grace, please have your way in me so that these characteristics of the Spirit overpower my own flesh. - Amen

"But each one is tempted when he is carried away and enticed by his own lusts. Then when lust is conceived, it gives birth to sin; and when sin is accomplished, it brings forth death."

James 1:14-15

Let's say you saw me about to take a drink from a glass that was tainted with poison - would I be upset if you stopped me? Let's say I was about to walk across a street that had an oncoming bus traveling towards me at a high rate of speed - would I be upset if you reached out to rescue me? Let's say I was about to step on a poisonous snake that I did not see - would I be angry that you pulled me back? No - I would be very thankful that you warned me or stopped me from all of these dangerous and deadly situations. So why is it that I get so angry or defensive when others warn me about sin? Maybe it is because I do not think that sin is really sin and I assume that it holds no sting for me. Or maybe I am deceived into thinking that sin in little doses will never hurt me. Oh God, help me today to recognize that every form of sin eventually hurts me and that those who warn me of this truth are the ones who really love me.

Dear Jesus,

Sometimes I choose to sin simply because I do not see the danger that lurks behind it. Please help me to realize that, even though my sins have been forgiven, continuing in them still poses a threat to my well-being. Give me the grace to choose obedience over sin. - Amen

"My speech and my preaching was not with enticing words."

1 Cor. 2:1-5

In my opinion, the Apostle Paul did more for the Christian church than anyone else in history apart from Jesus Christ. He wrote the majority of the New Testament, started churches all over the world and died passionately serving Christ. But he claimed that his work had nothing to do with him and that his message was not delivered with "enticing words". He was selling death to self - a marketing nightmare. But he was also communicating life eternal. He knew it was a hard sell, but he knew it was truth - so he gave his life to it. It just goes to show - you gotta believe in what you do, give God 100%. When you do what you do for the glory of God the results of His work through you will be phenomenal.

Dear Jesus,

Help me to not only live for you, but to passionately believe in what I am doing. Please help me, each day, to be filled with a burning desire for the things that concern you. - Amen

"I pray that out of His glorious riches He may strengthen you with power through His Spirit in your inner being."

Ephesians 3:16

Is there really anything that is impossible for the Christian to accomplish if it is the will of God? Every battle we face, every struggle we endure, every challenge we encounter - we confront them all with the power of God, given to us by God. There are many instructions given to me by God that I am tempted to identify as things "I can't" do: witness to a friend, forgive an enemy, accomplish a God given goal. However, the truth of the gospel is "I CAN" in Christ if it is something He would have me to do and be. It is not about me - it is all about Him. What is it that you are telling God that you can't do? If it is something that He is calling you too then isn't that in essence an insult to Him. Don't second guess the great things that God wants to accomplish through you.

Dear Jesus,

Help me to walk in your power today and to not let my human limitations and weaknesses identify my destiny. - Amen

"My house will be called a house of prayer."
Matthew 21:13

It was the Monday before the crucifixion and Jesus went to the temple where He found a lot of buying and selling happening instead of praying. It ticked Him off! Yes - Jesus got mad, so mad that he turned over all their tables and benches. What does this have to do with Holy Week? What made Jesus so mad? He was days away from the cross where He would be sacrificed for the sins of all men and now, just a few days before, He is witnessing the most holy place being turned into a mini-mall. These money changers were set up in the courts where the common man or woman would be able to attend the temple. Now the common man could not approach the temple in the one area designated for them because of all the clutter. And the ones who should have known better, were making the temple a place of personal gain rather than sacrificial worship. It begs the question for me today, am I standing in the way of someone coming into the presence of a Holy God or am I helping them find Him?

Dear Jesus,

Help me to live in such a way that I never get in the way of another man's worship because of my own selfishness. - Amen

"When the chief priests and the Pharisees heard Jesus'
parables they knew he was talking about them. They
looked for a way to arrest him,
but they were afraid of the crowd . . ."
Matthew 21:45-46

The Tuesday before Jesus' crucifixion is called the
"Day of Controversy" because of the exchange
between Jesus and the Pharisees. The religious
leaders were trying to discredit Jesus and Jesus
answered them through telling stories that they
understood to be condemning. Though these men
were considered leaders, they were still afraid to
publicly stand behind their claims for fear of the
crowd. Leadership and position are two totally
different concepts. A true leader does not fear the
reactions of the crowd, but instead they seek to
influence the actions of the crowd. They seek to

teach, not dictate. They seek to serve, not control. I like to think of the Tuesday before the crucifixion as "Leadership Day" for it was on this day that Jesus modeled to us how we can walk in confidence when we walk with God. And in so doing - we lead.

Dear Jesus,

I want to be a leader that makes a real difference in the world, but a leader that leads like you. Please, help me to never seek position or attention, but rather to seek to be in tune with you every day so that others can find their way to you. - Amen

"Now I know in part; then I shall know fully
even as I am fully known."
1 Corinthians 13:12

Nothing is revealed to us in the Scriptures concerning the Wednesday before the crucifixion. This day remains a mystery. To many it was just another day - mothers baking bread, fathers performing their trade, children playing in the dusty streets of Jerusalem. But God was at work. People were being used by the hand of God to prepare for the darkest yet most necessary moment in history and it was only a few days away. There are days when it seems that God is silent that maybe He has taken a break, but rest assured, God is never out to lunch - He is always working. Wednesday may have been quiet but our redemption was just a couple days away and the door to our eternity was beginning to crack open.

Dear Jesus,

Some days seem so common, so uneventful, so plain. Some days I can't really see how you are working in the basic routine of life. Please help me today to see that you are at work, no matter how exciting or common my day may be. - Amen

"I pray also for those who will believe in me through
their message."

John 17:20

The night before Jesus went to the cross, He was
praying for you. Just a few hours before his arrest,
Jesus was in the upper room with his disciples
giving them final instructions and He took a
moment to pray for me, for you and for all that
would believe on Him. We were present in the
upper room. Imagine that. You and I were in the
upper room. In the heart of God, we were there.
He was thinking of us, hoping for us and praying
for us. He prayed that we would be so united with
Him that the world would know the depth of His
love. Among the many images that we see
depicted of Jesus and the twelve disciples reclining
around a table of bread and wine in the upper

room, let's be sure to look a little deeper into those pictures and see a fourteenth person – ourselves, in the heart of God.

Dear Jesus,

The thought of you thinking of me and praying for me on the final night of your earthly life is humbling. Thank you Jesus for praying for me and for giving your all for me. Now help me to live in a way that shows the world your love.

- Amen

"Jesus said, 'It is finished.' With that, he bowed his head and gave up his spirit."

John 19:30

It was the project to beat all projects. From the moment Adam and Eve bit into the apple and sin entered the world, Almighty God began the process of reclaiming a relationship with His creation. For hundreds of years God would pursue humanity, not because He had to, not because He needed to, but all because He wanted to. He loved us too much to leave us in the desert of our sin. All along, He wanted us to live, to get back to that "perfect Eden", to be found right before Him so that we would not suffer. The project took years, a lot of patience and a Holy determination to not give up on us. So just before He breathed His last breath, from a brutal cross, Jesus said, "It is finished." In other words - Jesus was saying "mission accomplished, project complete, we made it, success, sin no longer has humanity in its grip, death does not even have the slightest sting, the war is over - WE WIN!

Dear Jesus,

Thank you, thank you, thank you for never giving up on us and for completing the project of destroying our sin. I love you Jesus.
THANK YOU! - Amen

"On the evening of that first day of the week, when the disciples were together, with the doors locked for fear of the Jews, Jesus came and stood among them and said, 'Peace be with you!'"

John 20:19

It was resurrection day! Just a few days prior, Jesus had been brutally murdered and all hope seemed to be gone for His followers. Now the disciples were tucked away in hiding in total despair - ON RESURRECTION DAY! I could understand them hiding on Friday night, even Saturday, but Sunday night? Especially after they had already been told that JESUS IS NOW ALIVE! Why would a disciple of Jesus fear anything if they knew He could conquer death itself? Hmmmmm. Good question. Why do we? It's easy for us to look at the disciples and say, "Come on guys! What are you so afraid of? That's Jesus! He is alive!" But we tend to cower behind locked doors of our own. We know Jesus is alive, but we still tremble in fear over the struggles of our lives. We assume that we are all alone, that it is up to us to find solutions to our problems. We fail to remember that Jesus is just as much alive today as He was on that first resurrection day. Do not fear! HE IS ALIVE and He lives inside of us!

Dear Jesus,

You are alive! You are alive! You are alive and you live in me! Help me today to keep this in mind. - Amen

"I will hear what God the Lord will speak:
for he will speak peace unto his people, and to his saints."
Psalm 85:8.

We take vitamins so that our bodies might fight off disease. We watch the weather report so that we can dress to protect ourselves from the elements of the day. We spend time exercising so that we might maintain a strong body. But do we make any effort to have healthy, peaceful minds? The Lord offers us His peace, but it only comes to us when we spend time alone with Him in His Word. Our salvation is a free gift. Our forgiveness is by grace alone. However, the peace of God that transcends all understanding will only consume our minds when we take the time to set our minds on the things of God and His Word. So today let's take our vitamins, put on a jacket, take a walk and spend a few moments in God's Word. Peace will surely come.

Dear Jesus,

Help me to draw from your Word the truths that will bring me peace of mind and a settled spirit. Jesus, I know peace will never come apart from you. Help me today to know you more and to experience your perfect peace. - Amen

"And I will wait for the Lord who is hiding His face from the house of Jacob; I will even look eagerly for Him."

Isaiah 8:17

Not many people enjoy waiting. No one seems to smile in long check-out lines. Most are not whistling happy tunes in rush hour traffic. Very few seem to find the brighter side of a few extra moments in the doctor's office. Waiting can be frustrating, especially when we are waiting on God. Where is He? When will He answer? Why is He taking so long? If you are waiting on the Lord today and it seems that He has hidden His face from you - take heart - He is not only the God who holds the answers, He is also the God who stands with you as you wait to see His plans unfold. As we wait with Him we discover that the answers we have been seeking are most often found in the actual struggle of the wait itself. Trust Him – even though you wait, He will not be late - He is always right on time.

Dear Jesus,

I can be so impatient at times; especially when I am waiting to hear from you or see you work. Jesus, please help me today to trust your timing and your power. I know you will not fail me. - Amen

"The Lord gives strength to his people;
the Lord blesses his people with peace."
Psalm 29:11

We always talk about how God has a great plan for our lives, but did you ever think about the fact that God has a great plan for our MINDS. Yes - God has a specific plan for us to live with total peace of mind. Think about it this way - have you ever driven past a beautiful house and said to yourself, "Wow! The electrical work in that house is incredible!" No - we usually only talk about the brick color or the beautiful porches, but never the wiring - because the wiring cannot be seen. But if it were not for the wiring, the house would remain dark on the inside - even if the exterior is beautiful. If God has a great plan for my life then he must also have a great plan for the inner workings of my thought life. He has a plan to "wire me" for peace. Total peace of mind is possible if we will walk in His ways and acknowledge Him in all we do. Set your mind on the Lord and His ways today and watch your house light up.

Dear Jesus,

Help me today to keep my mind set on you so that I can experience your peace. - Amen

*"But while he was still a long way off, his father saw
him and was filled with compassion for him; he ran to
his son, threw his arms around him and kissed him."*

Luke 15:20

Jesus tells a story of how a wayward son was
embraced by his father after the son had rebelled,
came to his senses and returned home. What a
beautiful picture of a father racing to embrace his
wayward son and welcome him home after a season
of rebellion and sin. But the most beautiful part of
this story is not so much in the story itself as much
as it is in the teller of the story. Jesus was the one
telling the story. Why would God in the flesh tell
such a story of grace unless He was eager to have
us understand how true it is? Every good teacher
knows how to illustrate their most important point
so that the students will get it. Jesus wants you to

get how much He loves you, how much He wants to embrace you, how eager He is to forgive you - that's why he told such a beautiful story of a wayward son being welcomed home. He wants you to know you are welcome with Him. What are you waiting for? Come home!

Dear Jesus,

Your love for me is incomprehensible. I often hear how you love me, but have a hard time really understanding it. Jesus, please help me to experience the love you have for me. I'm on my way home. - Amen

"You have made known to us the dream of the king."
Daniel 2:23

Daniel's back was against the wall. Nebuchadnezzer had a dream that no one could interpret so he called on Daniel for help. The pressure was on. If Daniel could not interpret the dream he would have been in a hot mess. His life was on the line. However, during the night, God revealed the meaning of the dream to Daniel - God told him all that he needed to know at just the right time. So Daniel was able to interpret Nebuchadnezzer's dream when no one else could. Sometimes life may seem a little unclear and hard to interpret, but as we walk with the Lord, He will reveal his purposes to us at just the right time. When He does, we will find ourselves living out the "dreams" of our King.

Dear Jesus,

When I try to figure out life on my own, I always come up short and confused. Please help me to always seek your wisdom so that I can experience the life that you have for me.
- Amen

"Lord, you established peace for us;
all that we have accomplished you have done for us."
Isaiah 26:12

Look over your life today. Examine all that is good.
Every big or little thing that brings you joy, that
settles your heart in peace, that brings a smile to
your face - that is God's handiwork, His gift to you.
It is not your work, it is His. It is not your
accomplishments, it is His through you. The bond
of a friend, the security of a roof, the warmth of a
family - all of these things that bring peace to our
lives are God accomplishments. When it feels like
peace may be far away, keep in mind that God is
working on new elements of peace to be established
into your life today. He is planning events,
relationships, opportunities and realities that will
bring a deep and settled peace into your life. He

has you in His hands and He will not let go. He is working on more peace and it is coming your way.

Dear Jesus,

Thank you for accomplishing peace into my life. Help me to realize that today you have more "peace plans" for me. Please, don't let me miss them.   - Amen

"Dear friends, do not be surprised at the painful trial you are suffering, as though something strange were happening to you."

1 Peter 4:12

Sometimes the Bible seems so ironic. In this passage Peter reminds the followers of Christ that they are not to be "surprised" when they go through difficult times. I think we can all agree that the very essence of a trial has an element of surprise to it every time. "I did not see that coming." or "I'm not sure what to do with that!" or just plain "YIKES!". How could Peter be so calm as he wrote of the suffering of Christians? Maybe he wasn't calm. Maybe he was just like me and you. Maybe he said these words after a sleepless night or during a time of great distress in his own life. From where he was standing Christians were suffering greatly (which included himself) and some even losing their lives (which eventually he did). Peter reminds us that suffering is to be expected and it is not a "strange" thing. It is actually pretty normal. Yet in every trial, God is able to see us through and to eventually lift us above the storm.

Dear Jesus,

It sure is hard to be thankful in times of suffering, but I know that there is no suffering that you cannot reach down into and show your power. Help me to experience your presence when I am hurting. - Amen

"An anxious heart weighs a man down,
but a kind word cheers him up."

Proverbs 12:25

According to this Proverb, it seems that relief from anxiety is brought only when we speak "kind words" to others, but what do you do when you are the one with the anxious heart? Are you left to wait for someone else to speak good into your life? Not necessarily. There is good news - the prescription of peace given in this verse is still available to you when you are the one with the anxious/heavy heart. It happens when you speak "kind words" to yourself. You can find peace when you speak to yourself the way that God speaks to you. As we speak the truth – "God loves me, He has a purpose for me and He will carry me", then we can feel the anxiety begin to lift off of our hearts. So today – speak kind to yourself and believe the "kind words" of Scripture - God loves you very much and will never abandon you or the purpose He has for you.

Dear Jesus,

Please help me to realize that the words I tell myself are very powerful. Please help me to be kind to myself so that I can experience your kindness to me. - Amen

"To the man who pleases him, God gives wisdom,
knowledge and happiness."
Ecclesiastes 2:26

Happiness seems to be the goal of every man and woman. Think about it, everything we choose is rooted in our quest for happiness. Our career, our mate, our friends, our hobbies, our home, our church, our clothes, our food (especially our food) - all these things are carefully selected with great hopes that they will make us happy. Solomon - who by the way was the wisest man that ever walked the face of the earth - looked back over his life and said that the only true happiness that he had ever known came from pleasing God. So often in Christian circles we hear how God will bring joy, but not always happiness, but I like to consider these words of Solomon that say that God is concerned with our happiness and He will bless us with lots of it if we will live to please Him. So I guess the old saying really is true - "Happiness is a choice." - a choice to please God in every area of life.

Dear Jesus,

I now happiness is not to be my goal in life, but I also know that you promise us a happy heart when we walk with you. Help me today to keep you in the center of all that I do today. Ultimately I know that will make me happy. - Amen

"When I said, 'My foot is slipping',
your love, O Lord, supported me."
Psalm 94:18

Once I tried ice skating with my kids. Most of the time I spent slowly shuffling my feet, keeping the wall within a few feet so I could crash onto it if need be. It was very slippery. It was also very obvious that most of the people there at the rink were in the same boat as I. People were crashing all around the rink. Why were we all so bad at it? Maybe because we were all natives of South Georgia. Not exactly ice skating territory. We were all outside of our normal environment of sandy beaches and palm trees. In this world, we as believers are like South Georgia ice skaters. We do not belong here. We have to struggle with things that God never intended for us to struggle with, yet they are now a part of this fallen world. Our

136

struggles are too difficult for us and it causes us to cry out - "I am slipping!" The good news is – when we cry out, the Lord is quick to run to our side and keep us from breaking our back over sin. He will catch us if we call. He will hold us up and safely bring us home to the environment we were made to enjoy – eternity with Him.

Dear Jesus,

Sometimes I get so tired of slipping and sliding in this world. Some days seem so uncertain. Remind me today that I do not belong here, but as long as I am here, I trust you to hold me up when I feel like I'm losing my footing. - Amen

"You have put all my sins behind your back."
Isaiah 38:17

What would happen if you tried driving to work today while looking only in the rearview mirror? I don't advise you to try it, but could you image how hard that would be. Imagine the intersections you would plunge through, the sidewalks you would hit, the other cars you would not see coming. Yep – driving by looking over your shoulder could be very dangerous. When we look in the rearview mirror, we lose focus of what is ahead of us. It puts us at greater risk of danger. It is much safer to look through the windshield and only glance back through the rearview mirror. We spend a lot of time in life looking in the rearview mirror at the failures of our past, but Jesus has forgiven them. If you are in Christ - every sin has been cancelled by

138

His work on the cross. He even puts them behind himself. If He does not dwell on them, then why do we? Today - admit that you have traveled down a few roads in life that were not the best for you. Ask the Lord to forgive you and set your sights through the windshield instead of the rear view mirror. We'll never enjoy the journey unless we look ahead and not behind.

Dear Jesus,

The mistakes of my past are too many to count, but the opportunities of my future far outweigh them. Help me today to crawl out from under that rock of condemnation, guilt and shame and to soar in the grace and love that you have for me. - Amen

"The grass withers, and the flower falls away,
but the word of the Lord endures forever."

1 Peter 1:24-25

The calendar changes daily, the weather changes hourly, paint fades, clothes tatter, food perishes, wealth is fickle, disappointment comes and goes, friends scatter, careers retire, moods change, feelings fluctuate and the earth itself slowly erodes. Everything changes - nothing stays the same, EXCEPT the Word of God. It will always be present to encourage, convict, comfort and guide. It is the anchor for the soul, the light for the darkness, the comfort for the downtrodden and the helper for the weak. Nothing can change it, alter it nor destroy it. It is constant. Today, don't let all the changes around you rattle you - rest in the one thing that never changes - God's Word.

Dear Jesus,

Everything around me changes. There is no guarantee in anything of this world, except you and your Word. Please help me to anchor my life in the only thing that is constant, the unchanging Word of God. - Amen

"How can a young man keep his way pure?
By living according to your word."

Psalm 119:9

Carpenters use them, seamstresses depend on
them, artists trust them - PATTERNS. Without a
pattern the finished product will always be
distorted. Tables will wobble because of uneven
legs, dresses will be ugly because of mismatching
sleeves and paintings may go unrecognizable.
God's Word is the pattern to our lives. It guides
us to the life that God has envisioned for us from
the beginning. Sadly though, we often use God's
Word as an accessory rather than a pattern. If you
want to experience the life God has for you, pattern
your life according to the Bible rather than trying
to pattern the Bible according to your life. In the

end, you will be more pleased with the finished product.

Dear Jesus,

Help me to stop trying to fit you into my plans. Help me to submit totally to your will and to your Word so that I may see the life pattern you have chosen for me. - Amen

"Reckless words pierce like a sword, but the tongue of the wise brings healing."

Proverbs 12:18

When my oldest son was younger he was obsessed with pocket knives. He begged and begged for a Swiss Army knife. He loved all the gadgets. For the longest time we would not let him have one and then finally we gave in at around age 10. Now he has a collection of them. However, each new knife brought with it a speech on how to use it. How to open it, close it, hold it, carry it and pass it without injuring anyone. I have to say, he is very responsible with them and very careful and so far there have been no injuries. It makes me wonder, what would the world be like if we carefully handled our tongues the way we carefully handle pocket knives. Just a thought.

Dear Jesus,

My tongue is a dangerous weapon when not submitted to you, but a fountain of blessing when it is. Before I step out of the house today, I submit my tongue to you. Please use it for blessing and not cursing. - Amen

"So keep up your courage, ..."

Acts 27:25

In the 1950s, Elizabeth Elliot, wife of missionary
Jim Elliot who was killed by a tribe of Acca
Indians, felt called by God to minister to these
natives that had killed her husband. However, she
was very afraid to follow this call - as anyone
would be. While sharing her fears with a friend,
her friend told her "Do it afraid." This compelled
her to follow through with God's call on her life,
even though she felt great fear. As a result,
Elizabeth Elliot led the tribe that she once feared
to place their faith in Christ. Courage is not the
absence of fear - it is the ability to keep moving
ahead, even when fear grips our hearts. If you are
afraid today, know that there is nothing that God
cannot see you through. Trust Him and keep
moving ahead, even if you feel fear. Have courage

and "Do it afraid." Eventually God will subside those fears.

Dear Jesus,

Please do not let fear hinder me from accomplishing the great things you have in store for my life. Please give me courage to face every challenge of today with confidence and peace. - Amen

". . . no good thing does he withhold from those whose walk is blameless."

Psalm 84:11

Sometimes we confuse God's unconditional love with his conditional blessings. Nowhere in the Bible does it ever suggest that God blesses a person or a nation that walks outside of His will. If He withholds nothing from those who walk blameless, then it only stands to reason that He does withhold blessings from those who do not. Salvation is free, God's love is unconditional, but His blessings only fall on us when we walk in His ways. He knows we are sinful, that is why He came to save us. He knows we are weak, that is why He gave us His Spirit to empower us. He knows we are incapable of making wise choices on our own, that is why He gives us the mind of Christ. These spiritual truths should not become excuses for walking our own path apart from Him and expecting God to bless it. He expects us to obey and walk in His ways. When we do, He rewards us. When we don't, He holds back those blessings. As you start your day, be determined in the Spirit to walk in His ways, no matter how you feel, and watch His blessings come to you.

Dear Jesus,

Help me never to confuse grace with a license to freely sin without conscience. Thank you for your grace – now help me to live a life that shows you how grateful I am for what you have done for me. - Amen

"For you died, and your life is now
hidden with Christ in God."
Colossians 3:3

There are mornings when I would like to just pull the covers up over my head and hide. It just seems a lot more comfortable, a lot safer and a whole lot easier to just hide from the world instead of face the challenges that it holds. Hiding under a warm blanket on a cold morning just seems like the most logical choice, but it is not an option. I can't hide in bed all day, but I can hide in Christ. Whatever the day throws as me, I can pull the covers of Christ over my heart and let Him guide me, comfort me and strengthen me for the task. Under His cover I am safe, free and at peace. Whatever you are facing today just know that you are hidden in Christ - so rest.

Dear Jesus,

You are the great comforter, my shield and my protector. Give me courage to face those days that I would rather avoid. Give me strength to stand when my strength seems to be fading. Give me confidence to trust you when things seem unclear. Give me peace in the shelter of your mighty powerful hand. - Amen

"I am convinced that nothing can ever separate us from His love."

Romans 8:38

God's love for you is stubborn, it will not be chased away. His love for you is constant, it knows no end. His love for you is steady, you can do nothing to shake it. His love for you is deep, it runs deeper than any love you have ever known or felt. His love for you is perfect, it lacks nothing. His love for you is painful, it hurts Him to discipline you. His love for you is complete, it meets every need in your soul. His love for you is powerful, it can chase away your greatest fears. His love for you is rich, it has secured an inheritance for you in a Kingdom that will never fade. His love for you is strong, it cannot be swayed, shaken nor destroyed. His love for you is real - don't let doubt cause you to reject it.

Dear Jesus,

Your love for me is incomprehensible, but I pray today that I might grasp just a taste of it. I love you, Jesus. - Amen

"God causes all things to work together for good ... "

Romans 8:28

This verse means nothing without that simple three letter word – "ALL". ALL means ALL, nothing is left out, nothing is irrelevant, nothing is outside of the powerful hand of God. Our challenges as well as our successes, our heartaches as well as our joys, He uses it all. Before the creation of the world, God knew every experience that you and I would face today and how each experience would be woven into the tapestry of our lives. He makes no mistakes and leaves nothing unused. There are no leftovers with God. No scraps lying on the floor. No parts unused. He uses it all and He works it all together for the good of those who love Him. Yes- God is busy working on your life and what He is working on will bring you much joy.

Dear Jesus,

Help me today to see how you are always working to fashion a life for me that I could never fashion for myself. A life that is good and pleasing to you and to me. – Amen

"Even though I walk through the valley of the shadow of death, I will fear no evil, for you are with me."

Psalm 23:4

Psalm 23 is a great passage of comfort and assurance that God is with us, but it was written from a heart that was struggling. David begins with the assurance that he knew God was leading Him to green pastures, quiet waters and paths of righteousness, but he was also anxious over the shadow of death - the prospect of danger - the fear of the unknown. However, a shadow cannot hurt you. It only reminds you that the object of that shadow is close by. Because He knew God, death could never touch David, but the fears associated within its shadow could. If you are facing uncertain times, difficult decisions or maybe even the fear of death itself, know that you are only in its shadow and if you are hidden in Christ, He will lead you, empower you and protect you. Remember - shadows never hurt us and light makes them disappear.

Dear Jesus,

Many fears are found in the shadows, fears of the unknown that lurk in the dark. Jesus, you have brought light into the darkness. Today I need you to chase the fears and shadows away and to help me walk in the light. - Amen

". . . without Me you can do nothing" [Jesus]
John 15:5

Every day we choose the things that we will surrender to God and the things that we will not. We tend to give Him the huge things like, "Lord heal this sickness or bring world peace." But we do not give Him the little things like "Lord help me to have a better attitude or to keep my mind from worry." But John writes that we can do NO thing apart from Him. I cannot fully forgive, freely love or unconditionally serve without Christ in me. He is essential for all things good done for me, in me and through me. The more I realize this, the more I am compelled to worship Him out of a heart that is dependent and thankful. As you start your day, keep in mind that all things are possible for you, but only with the power of God working within you.

Dear Jesus,

I try so hard to control every aspect of my life, but the more I try to gain control, the more my life spins out of control. Jesus, I can do nothing without you, but with you – the sky is the limit. Help me to surrender totally to you. - Amen

". . . being confident of this, that he who began a good work in you will carry it to completion until the day of Christ Jesus."
Philippians 1:6

My parents always taught me that I should finish what I start. We were never allowed to quit a team in the middle of the season, whatever toys we pulled out we had to put up and if we made a promise to a friend we had to follow through. However, if I am honest, there are some insignificant projects that I start that never get finished. There are times when my good intentions outweigh my ability to deliver. A dresser that was never completely refinished, a picture that was never framed, a lawn mower that was never repaired. I am so thankful that God has no projects left on the shelf or good intentions unfulfilled. He is always working and working for our good and He will not stop until His purpose in us is complete.

Dear Jesus,

Thank you for never giving up on me. Thank you for patiently and consistently working on my life to bring about your purpose for me. - Amen

"... clothe yourselves with humility toward one another."

1 Peter 5:5

I believe Mary and Joseph were very strong people. I also believe that they were both very humble people. As a matter of fact, I believe that their strength came from their humility. Could you imagine the Christmas story without humility? I could hear Joseph now at the inn keeper's door, "Are you kidding me! No Room! Do you have any idea who you are talking to?! This woman is carrying God in her womb! I want to speak to the manager!" How about Mary? "Joseph, you would think, considering my condition, that you could have come up with something better than a donkey to travel on to Bethlehem!" (which by the way, we assume the donkey). Imagine the bickering, the whining, the pity-parties. But God would have

162

never chosen prideful people for this great task - He rarely ever does. Out of Mary and Joseph's humility we see God do a great miracle - a Savior is born. Let's keep this in mind as we approach the crunch of Christmas. Humility is always the formula for strength and most often the prelude to miracles.

Dear Jesus,

I often overlook the power of humility and how you choose to use those who live with humble spirits. Dear Jesus, please help me to put the interests of others before my own and to seek you over my own desires. Empower me to live in humility that I might bring honor to you. - Amen

"... he who watches over you will not slumber."

Psalm 121:3

Have you ever thought about the fact that God has
never had a good night's sleep. Of course, He does
not need it, but isn't that astounding? It is very
comforting to know that the God who created me,
watches over me 24/7 and He never needs a break.
He never dozes off, never needs a nap, never gets
cranky because He's tired, never shuts His eyes
temporarily taking His attention away from me. He
does not miss a thing. Even while I sleep, He
watches and His attention to me does not waiver
throughout the night and all through the day. Why
is He so attentive? I think you know the answer.
We focus on the things we love. WE are enamored
with the things that interest us. We are protective
of the things we create. We are fascinated with the

things that have our deepest affections. Yes- God
never sleeps, because He just can't take His eyes off
of us.

Dear Jesus,

**Sometimes it is hard to understand how
attentive you are to me. Please, help me to see
the depth of your love and to experience the
comfort of your presence. - Amen**

"He [Jesus] went to Nazareth, where he had been
brought up, . . ."
Luke 4:16

Jesus began his ministry in his own hometown, in the streets where he played as a child, among family and friends. Just after his baptism and his temptation in the desert, Matthew tells us that Jesus went home to begin teaching and preaching the incredible message of salvation - at home. It does not matter how far we go in life, the successes we achieve, the recognition we receive - if we have not ministered to the people under our own roof first - we have failed. Be intentional today about your faith at home. Before you encourage your neighbor, encourage your spouse. Before you teach a Bible Study at church, have a devotion with your kids in their rooms. The mission field is calling you - and it is sitting at your breakfast table.

Dear Jesus,

Under my roof is a mission field. Within my own family is a congregation. Jesus, please help me to reach out by reaching in and to show your love to the ones who are closest to me. - Amen

"He who walks with the wise grows wise, but a companion of fools suffers harm."

Proverbs 13:20

People are like sponges. Whether we like it or not, we absorb our surroundings and we become the people that we embrace. When we choose our friends and companions we are in essence deciding our own destiny. Just take a look at your phone log and review the most frequently called friends and family – that's you. You will find yourself in those people. Sometimes we are not very selective with our closest companions and we make unwise choices. We fool ourselves if we think that we can choose negative environments and come forth as positive people. Do you want a good assessment of the kind of person you really are? Look at the people around you - the ones you choose to embrace. Most likely you will find that you are those people. So choose wise companions who love the Lord and seek His will and see if it doesn't enrich your life.

Dear Jesus,

You call me to love all people, but you instruct me to be careful who I pattern my life after. Help me to identify wise and Godly people and then to align myself with them. - Amen

"Do not answer fools according to their folly,
or you will be a fool yourself."

Proverbs 26:4

Having the last word does not always mean that you have to have the last word. Sometimes the best way to deal with a difficult person is to smile and move on. What good will it do for you to argue? Do you think you will win? If you "win" in an argument with a fool have you really won? Even if you "win" in words - you may lose in character. So is it worth it? Does it really pay off for you to walk away from an argument having shot down another person with your words? Has it enriched their life? No – it just made them mad. Has it enriched your life? No – it just lowered you to a level of childlike immaturity. If it is the wise man that knows when to shut his mouth then what does it say about me when I keep running mine?

Dear Jesus,

Please help me to understand that you are the only one with the authority to have the last word in every situation. Guard my tongue today and let my words be few. - Amen

"Weeping may endure for a night,
but joy cometh in the morning."
Psalm 30:5

Did you go to bed with a heavy heart? Was your mind consumed with worry or fear? Is your pillow stained with tears from a night of weeping? Be encouraged this morning - the Lord has hit the reset button. It is a new day. He has pulled the sun up again; He has given you air to breath and countless blessings that await you. Life is hard – I agree. Sometimes it's hard to see past the heartaches, but God encourages us to leave yesterday's tears in yesterday and to embrace a hopeful outlook on today. Your circumstances may be the same -but so is your God. He will never change - He is always good, always loving, always in control. So leave the pains of last night in the dark and move out into today's joyful sunrise.

Dear Jesus,

Yesterday may have been rough, but this morning I choose to receive your joy. – Amen

"Give thanks in all circumstances."

1 Thessalonians 5:18

These words of Paul were not taken from an ancient greeting card. These were words spoken by a man who had been run out of the city by an angry mob because of his preaching, he had been beaten, imprisoned and shipwrecked - all because of His faith. In the midst of it all he never cried, "That's not fair!" or "I don't deserve this!" He viewed all of life through one lens -Jesus Christ. Paul never said, "give thanks FOR all circumstances" - he said, "give thanks IN all circumstances." He proves that thankfulness is a choice. Living thankfully made Paul a stronger, better person and gave Him the strength to endure many hardships. Today, let's live thankful and experience the peace of God in every area of our lives.

Dear Jesus,

I admit that I complain way too much. Help me today to have an attitude of thanksgiving rather than a selfish, negative spirit. - Amen

"The Lord confides in those who fear him."

Psalm 25:14

Only the best of friends confide in one another. They share their deepest thoughts and their greatest dreams. Confiding in a friend strengthens my heart, but having a friend confide in me is even better. It makes me feel important, trusted and valued. To have someone confide in you is the greatest compliment. It means that they value you enough to tell you their deepest thoughts and dreams. The Psalmist writes that the Lord confides in those who love Him. Wow! Almighty God confides in us. Not for direction, but for intimacy. Though God does not confide in me for advice (thank goodness), I pray He will confide in me with His great hopes and dreams for my life as I respect and fear Him. Wouldn't it be great to be best friends with the Lord? It is possible.

Dear Jesus,

Teach me to always keep my door open for you to come in and confide in me. - Amen

"Going a little farther, he fell to the ground and prayed that if possible the hour might pass from him."

Mark 14:35

The agony of the cross was so overwhelming that even Jesus had moments of wondering if He was going to make it any farther. In a moment of deep anguish and gut-wrenching prayer, Jesus cried out to His Father and asked, "Is there any way around this?!" But eventually that night, to the sound of approaching soldiers, Jesus pulled Himself up out of the dirt, brushed the sweat from his brow, wiped the tears off of His face and pushed through his greatest fear. When He was at His darkest moment He "went a little farther". Because He was willing to go "a little farther", He was able to push through and put death to death. When you get discouraged just keep going "a little farther" in the Lord's direction and you will soon find peace.

Dear Lord,

So often I am tempted to stop short of the goals you have placed before me. Help me today to go "a little farther" and see your glory. - Amen

"I sought the Lord, and He heard me, and delivered me from all my fears."

Psalm 34:4

Read this verse again, but slow down. - Now read it again even slower. Does anything jump out at you? How about "He heard me". It is a great comfort to know that God has the power to subside our fears, but the even greater truth is that "He hears me". I have Almighty God's attention. When I pray, He hears. His line is never busy. His reception is always clear. He will never put me on hold. He hears the smallest utterance of my heart. When I feel like a speck of insignificant dust on a giant globe filled with millions of people - God almighty hears me. He hears when I am afraid and He comes to my rescue. He hears when I cry for answers. He hears when I have worries. He hears when I ask for direction. He hears me - and He brings peace.

Dear Jesus,

I believe that you can hear me – so please hear me now when I say, I need you to meet me where I am so that my soul may find rest. - Amen

"If I were still trying to please men,
I would not be a servant of Christ."
Galatians 1:10

I must hear this at least five times a day from my little girl, "Daddy, watch this!!" It is usually followed with some type of gymnastics front tuck or a homemade cheer routine. And what do I do? I watch, applaud and say "WOW! That was great!" Why? Because I am the father and that is what father's do. Nothing makes a father happier than when his child asks for his attention and does something to try and impress him. And I've noticed that when a father gives affirmation, it brings the biggest smiles. Today, make your heavenly Father your only audience. Don't seek to please everyone around you. Quite frankly, they don't care as much for you as He does and they cannot make you feel as secure as He can. He has your best interest at heart. He wants to see you succeed. He loves you with a love you cannot fathom. Do every "flip" for Him today and don't worry about what others may think. In the end keep in mind, your heavenly Father does not love you because of what you do, He loves you because He is your Daddy. You make Him smile.

Dear Jesus,

I pray that today will be a day when I do not worry about the opinions of others, but instead I simply live to please you. I pray that my life today will bring joy to your heart and a smile to your face. - Amen

"Trust in him at all times, . . ."

Psalm 62:8

What do you do when those around you praise the Lord for giving them a job, but you are still left unemployed? You trust. What do you do when your friend gives thanks for a baby, but your arms are still empty? You trust. What do you do when a family member celebrates a good doctor report, but you are still sick? You trust. What do you do when you move out of your home to follow the Lord, but the house you left won't sell? You trust. Sometimes God does not move in ways that we expect Him to move. Sometimes God does not act in ways that we think He should act. Sometimes God does not change the things that we want Him to change. But one thing is for sure, He is always right in what He does. And so we trust.

184

Dear Jesus,

We are so quick to give you praise when good things happen, but so slow to give you praise when life does not work out the way we think it should. Help me to praise you in the good times and the bad. I totally trust you. - Amen

"The Lord says, I will guide you along the best pathway for your life. I will advise you and watch over you."

Psalm 32:8

One summer I went rafting with my son in the Tennessee mountains. We had a choice to either go on our own or to have a guide in the boat with us. Since I had only been rafting a couple of times before this trip and I was not very experienced on the river, we opted for the guide. He knew every turn of the river. He knew the most dangerous rapids before we approached them and he knew the safest places for us to jump out and play in the water. If I can't go down a river without a guide, what makes me think I can navigate this complicated life without one. As I journey through life, I have found that it is better to opt for the raft with the guide especially when that guide is the Lord.

Dear Jesus,

Life is filled with rapid waters and unexpected turns. Please help me to always seek your guidance and to never try and navigate my life on my own. Guide me today by your wisdom.
- Amen

"God is light; in him there is no darkness."

1 John 1:5

I'm never surprised to find a fish wet or a pig muddy. I'm never surprised to see that a flower grows in the sun or dies in the dark. I'm never caught off guard when a raindrop falls from a dark cloud or a bird soars against the wind. Why - because they are all products of their environment. Surroundings determine outcome. So why am I surprised when humans lie to get ahead, steal to take advantage, or kill to gain control? Dark results come from dark environments. Since the fall of Adam and Eve this world has been a dark kingdom. So rather than look at humanity and become enraged at the obvious darkness in our actions, I acknowledge that we all live in a very dark environment that tends to rub off on us. Yet -

the good news is that Jesus can help us to walk in the light and give daily evidence that He has overcome our dark environment. And when we walk with Him - we will most certainly look like fish out of water.

Dear Jesus,

Help me to stop trying to change a pagan culture into something that it is not. Help me to walk so closely with you that I will obviously be out of place in this fallen world. – Amen

"But the Lord is in his holy temple;
let all the earth be silent before him."
Habakkuk 2:20

Some of the most meaningful times that I have had
with my kids have been in total silence. Just this
morning, while I was having a cup of coffee on the
couch, my little girl wandered into the living room
in her PJs. With sleepy eyes and crazy hair bed
head, she curled up on the couch with me. Not a
word was said. Not the usual curious questions
about life. No pleas for help with dealing with her
brothers. No requests for a drink of water or help
with getting dressed. She asked for nothing. She
was just with me, cuddled up under my arm. It
made me realize - God desires the same from me.
With God as my Father, I know that I can take
every need of my life to Him and He will meet

them in His time and in His way. But there are times when all He wants from me is for me to sit in His presence and not say a word. So that's what I did today. My morning prayer was not about anything or for anyone - It was just sitting silently in the presence of Jesus - and it was one of the most meaningful times with God that I have had.

Dear Jesus,

Today I ask nothing of you. I just want to sit with you. – Amen

"God demonstrates His own love toward us,
in that while we were sinners, Christ died for us."

Romans 5:8

I've heard this verse most of my life. Read it, quoted it, and even preached on it, but have somehow always overlooked a very important word in it . . . "DEMONSTRATED". To "demonstrate" means to display, to show off, to highlight something that needs to have the attention of others. I have no problem understanding that I'm a sinner and I am grateful that Christ died for me while I was in that state, but realizing that the reason He did it was to display, make known, highlight how great is His love for me makes me feel valuable. If you have ever said, "God, show me that you love me.", know that He already has "demonstrated" it in a very powerful way – on a nasty Roman cross in Jerusalem.

Dear Jesus,

You could have demonstrated your love for me in many ways, but no other way could touch the depth of your love like your sacrifice on the cross. Thank you for that. I love you. - Amen

". . . our compentence comes from God."

2 Corinthians 3:5

Do you ever doubt yourself? Do you ever look around you and see "successful" people and wonder why your life seems so mediocre? Do you ever wish you could accomplish something great and meaningful but just feel like you do not have what it takes? Well, you are in good company. Most people feel that way at some point in life, but there is a way to overcome it. Rather than looking at what you cannot do, try looking at what God can do through you. If Almighty God can form the earth from His hands and mold the human race from a lump of clay, He can surely make you competent to accomplish great things in life. But His "great things" are not always our "great things". Our "great things" are power, possessions and praise - all for ourselves. His "great things" are service, loving others and genuine worship. Stop beating yourself up - see how God has made you competent and live a full life.

Dear Jesus,

I am my own worst critic. Sometimes I look around me and feel so insignificant in the world. Help me today to realize that you created me for a purpose and that you can do great things through me - things that others may view as insignificant, but things that you would view as great. - Amen

"Give thanks to the Lord, for he is good.
His love endures forever."
Psalm 136:1

When I was a kid there was one thing that I could always count on, one thing that always endured, one thing that never changed - no matter what was going on in the world. No matter how I behaved or did not behave. No matter if I felt good or bad, happy or sad. No matter the weather, the president, the culture or the mood - there was one thing that was always consistent - my grandmother's cookie jar was always full. Whether my visit was announced or unannounced, somehow that little jar on her kitchen table was always gushing with goodies like a bottomless fountain of eternal sugar and it always made me feel good when she would lead me to it. She was always prepared with something good for her grandkids. Did you know that God has something good for you today? It is sitting there on His table. All He asks is that you visit with him for just a moment so that He can give you some of His consistent and unchanging love that will never run out. Take a moment and reach into the jar of His goodness. It will make you feel good.

Thank You Munty & Thank You Jesus!

Dear Jesus,

Thank you that your goodness never runs out. Lead me to the "jar" of your blessings every day and help me to lead others to partake as well. - Amen

"Behold, I am the Lord, the God of the flesh:
is there anything too hard for me?"
Jeremiah 32:27

Our deepest struggles come not from wondering if God CAN, but rather wondering if God WILL. We believe that He is able to do anything but that makes the seasons of waiting that much harder. "God, why haven't you fixed it, healed it, made it go away!?" "God, when will you answer, provide or intervene since I know you can?!" Waiting on the Lord can be a crucible of pain, but it is the process through which we learn to trust Him. Without the wait we would never really know who He is and how much He really loves us and is working for our good. So today, look over your shoulder and see the faithfulness of God in your past and then look ahead and know that nothing is too difficult for Him.

Dear Jesus,

I know you can do all things, but sometimes I wonder why you won't do certain things. No matter what you do, I trust you completely. Forgive my doubts, fears and frustrations. Help me to rest in you. - Amen

"Pride only breeds quarrels,
but wisdom is found in those who take advice."
Proverbs 13:10

When was the last time you admitted that you were wrong? No seriously - think about it - when was the last time you misspoke and had to eat crow, you overreacted and had to apologize, you failed to keep a promise and had to ask for forgiveness? If it has been a while since you have had to admit that you were wrong then you may have an issue with pride. Or I guess it's possible that you are always right and never make any mistakes - but not very likely. The strongest among us are the men and women who humbly admit when they make a mistake, who are more concerned with honesty than they are with

popularity. Be strong today - go low to go high.
Admit your mistakes.

Dear Jesus,

Help me never to be so consumed with being right that I live a life that is wrong. Help me to own up to my mistakes – to live in humility and with integrity. - Amen

"Love never fails."
1 Corinthians 13:8

It is one of my earliest childhood memories. Every afternoon, Mama would be in the kitchen cooking dinner and Daddy would walk in the back door from work wearing a blue uniform with his name on it. He did not stop to talk to us, he did not go to another room to change clothes, he did not plop down on the couch or turn on the TV. No – the first thing he did, every night, was to go straight to my Mama and give her a kiss. I saw that nearly every day of my childhood. I never realized what an impact it had made on me until I was sitting in my parents kitchen just a few months ago. You see, my Mama cannot remember things like she did years before. Her mind is fading. Sometimes she even forgets my Daddy's name. But at the age of

202

43 I was sitting in their kitchen talking to her when my Daddy walked in the back door and instinctively he walked over to give her a kiss and she puckered up. Yep – this old world can try all it wants to steal from us, but love – true love never fails and I am eternally grateful.

Dear Jesus,

Thank you for giving me a Mama and Daddy that still kiss hello. - Amen

"In my Father's house are many rooms. If it were not so,
I would have told you, I go to prepare a place for you?"

[Jesus]

John 14:2

Do you remember what it was like as a child to be afraid of the dark? Bedtime was like a horror movie. We would check under the bed for monsters and stare at the closet door to be on guard against the "boogie man". We would try to be brave, but some nights were harder than others, so we would often call in for reinforcements - Mamma or Daddy. Nothing would make us go to sleep faster than just having a parent lay next to us. With the comfort of their presence, all seemed to be well and we would drift off to sleep, clutching our favorite blankie or worn out teddy bear.

However, there were times when we would wake in the middle of the night to find that Mama or Daddy were not there any longer. In those times, panic would overcome us. Our parents had not abandoned us, they simply were *in the next room.*

As children, we did not realize that our parents were within reach. All we knew was that we felt all alone, because of that we were overcome with anxiety and fear. We felt completely vulnerable to the monsters under the bed and the "boogie man" in the closet. Yet, the whole while, Mama and Daddy were just a cry away, *in the next room.*

When we lose someone we love, we often feel like that little child in the dark. We feel vulnerable, lost, abandoned, afraid, alone. But what we must realize is that we have not lost them at all, they are simply *in the next room.*

There is no greater joy than to watch our children run into our bedrooms with each new day as they jump into our beds with an excitement that seems to say, "I made it through the night!". We laugh and play and we wrestle around in the bed before we begin our new day together. It is a celebration of the new day that has dawned.

In our times of grief, we must remind ourselves that our dawn is yet to come. One day we too will enter into *the next room* and we will see those that we love. We will laugh and talk and play as we celebrate that we made it through the night. We will not feel vulnerable, afraid or even concerned any longer. We won't hurt, we won't cry, we won't argue, we won't die. We will just gather with those who have gone before us at the feet of our Heavenly Father who prepared a place for us *in the next room.*

So when those we love pass on, let's not say "goodbye", but instead let's say, "I'll see you in the morning." For we know that sorrow lasts only for a night, but joy – oh unspeakable joy – joy comes in the morning.

Written for Angus Clinton Zittouer "Uncle Clinton" - 2002

Scripture references from The Holy Bible.

.

Made in the USA
Charleston, SC
15 March 2014